Take to the Highway:
Arabesques for Travelers

some other works by

Bryce Milligan

poetry

Daysleepers & Other Poems (1984)
Litany Sung at Hell's Gate (1990)
From Inside the Tree (recording, 1990)
Working the Stone (1993)
Alms for Oblivion: A Poem in Seven Parts (2003)
Lost and Certain of It (2006)
Recasting (2011)

young adult fiction

Battle of the Alamo (1990, 1999)
Comanche Captive (1990, 2005)
Lawmen: Stories of Men Who Tamed the West (1994)
With the Wind, Kevin Dolan (1987, 1990)
Kevin Dolan (German ed., 1994)

children's books

Brigid's Cloak: An Ancient Irish Story (2002)
*The Prince of Ireland
and the Three Magic Stallions* (2003)

books edited

¡Floricanto Sí! A Collection of Latina Poetry (1998)
*Daughters of the Fifth Sun: A Collection of Latina
Fiction and Poetry* (1995)
This Promiscuous Light (1995)
et al.

Take to the Highway

Arabesques for Travelers

Poems and prose poems

Bryce Milligan

West End Press
Albuquerque, New Mexico
2016

Take to the Highway: Arabesques for Travelers © 2016 by Bryce Milligan

Cover photograph by the author.

Quotation from "Country Road" by James Taylor,
1970 © by Sony/ATV Music Publishing LLC. By permission.

Printed in the United States of America

First Print Edition September 2016
ISBN: 978-0-9970353-0-8

Ebooks:
ePub: 978-1-60940-513-7
Kindle/mobipocket: 978-1-60940-514-4
Library PDF: 978-1-60940-515-1

West End Press
P.O. Box 27334
Albuquerque, NM 87125

For book information, see our web site at
www.westendpress.org

Milligan, Bryce.
  [Poems. Selections]
  Take to the Highway : Arabesques for Travelers / Bryce Milligan.
    pages ; cm
  ISBN 978-0-9970353-0-8 (pbk. : alk. paper) -- ISBN 978-1-
60940-513-7 (epub ebook) -- ISBN 978-1-60940-514-4 (kindle-
mobipocket ebook) -- ISBN 978-1-60940-515-1 (library pdf
ebook)
  I. Title.
  PS3563.I42283 T35 2016.
  811'.54

CONTENTS

I. Elevation's the New Salvation

II. Take to the Highway
(Prose poems written at speed)

III. All That Would Be

for Brigid,
storykeeper, planet-saver

I.

Elevation's the New Salvation

Prelude for Siduri

She wears her blues
like Shiva's skin,
courts the shoreline
of an ocean that once
when she was still
in love with it
bit her on the heel
and thus revealed
even sun and surf
envy the freedom
she alone can bare
before the gods
of her small sea.

Lost Lines

Words prance across
the blinding windshield
like appaloosa ponies
headed from their dim
night-shadowed canyons
onto the sage plain

the cadence rising—words,
words like hoofbeats—
as the herd hits
clear sunlit plains,
the playground plains,
el Llano Estacado

flat, so flat,
good ground for
running, running, running.
Brown and white and gold
they blaze and vanish
into the sun.

One More Brief Encounter

A distant glimpse of crimson fades at dusk
beyond the placid surface shifting blue
to gray, beyond the shadowed bridge where brusque
policemen watch headlights skitter and skew
the rippled mirror till they too are gone.
Her crimson dress dissolves to gray at last
yet her moment's grace on the shore's long lawn
stays in the mind as if a shadow cast
by a restless heart on a windless night,
a city's hymn to its stagnant river.
A shadow's shadow swallows all the light.
No sharp silhouette, only a shiver
dances among the dimming leaves as she
slips from the red dress into memory.

Virginia Pines

for Hermine

Vine-laced Virginia pines line the highway,
century-old sentries, dark against the dawn.

Sharp as obsidian shards—Clovis points
arranged in rank on serried razor rank—

the treetops' saw-teeth rip the starless dark
and dawn bleeds all along the horizon,

defining, refining her dark and lovely woods.

High Country Caravan

for Mary; in memory of Steve Frumholz

We drive a thousand miles
out of the sodden south
for this, the swish,

the whispers in the big sage,
murmurs in the piñones
and the highland pines

that rise above the scrub,
lifting their dark
and drowsy crowns

in an acclamation of elegance.
Your shadow-dappled arms
draw me higher still

off on a high country caravan
singing the old songs again
seeking the silver-shaking aspen.

West of Lampasas

for T.J. Poole

I sought the crumbled limestone crown
of this middling hill with no reason
beyond it being taller than its mate
across the way, when a path—glimpsed
through scrub oak and cedar—lured me
toward some imagined sunny height

even as the gulley-riven slope pulled
my steps toward the arroyo that runs,
when it runs, off toward Little School Creek.
But then a lane emerged beyond a fall
of storm-wasted cedar, rounded
the hill then cut straight

across the tangled landscape
—a private road, not the county's—
recently strewn with crushed marble
almost too white to walk on.
Further on, aging elms
embowered the narrow lane

barely wider than a wagon path
but lacking ruts or other marks
of human passage, I could not
but wonder who had renewed
with glistening stone
a path so antique, older

than the present generation,
older than our grandfathers,
and so, though it was not my labor
I made it my path for the day
until the alley opened out
onto an empty meadow.

Birthplace? Deathplace?
Homeplace? No carved stone,
no threshold or hearth,
no rude cross gave a hint.
Only the path told how
this land had been loved.

Another Visitation

Old Joaquin's seen the future.
She came to him last night,
one shoulder bare, hair affright,
sandy-sandaled and ocean-eyed.
He says he came back to tell us all.
"I shall tell you all," he said,
completamente formal,
next morning at the Taquería del Sol.

He couldn't get over how the graceful
young century's eyes brimmed
con nuestros dolores, tiempos, y las mareas—
tides that will not wait, cannot wait
to drown the barrier islands
and creep across the coastal plains
bringing the breakers to La Paloma Solitaria,
turning cotton fields and orange orchards
into salt marshes, arroyos into bayous.
"It'll be sandy soon enough," she told Joaquin.

He sold his truck that very week,
bought concrete and creosoted timbers.
"Elevation's the new salvation"
he'd repeat mantra-like
as he sank shafts through the alluvium
to the bed rock, poured foundations
for twenty-foot piles that soared up
like stilt legs stalking the future
in his pasture's chaparral.

Earth-bound

They're ripping out the rusted rails:
the gravel track-bed snakes away
ribbed with troughs of absent ties
that catch the stormy night's remains
to burn as mirrored rungs at dawn
as if Jacob's ladder had come
asunder with some wild desire
and fallen blessed with angel's fire.

Rain in Due Season

West of the highway, against the dusky
green and seemingly immortal cedars,
the drought-scoured sycamores stand naked
months before their time, their white limbs
almost grotesque, whiter than sun-bleached
driftwood, white as only clouds should be,
whiter than dry bones and yet unwithered—
stark but sturdy, sun-stunned but sun proof
as the living sap inside abides.

The Green Man Returns to Greenland

Newly calved, the shards of ancient glaciers
ride toward deeper waters, darker waters,
beginning to melt even as the sea
surrounds them, lapping fresh water wounds
with salty tongues that cannot staunch
the molecular awakening.
Sunlight and ice yield virgin springs,
freed at last from millennia of placid,
frozen dreams, cascading in crystal
rainbowed streams into the gray waves.

Ashore, stones split, crack with sharp
hallelujahs in sunlight so long denied;
the frozen droppings of a thousand
generations of puffins and gulls, seals and hares
steam and team with the brilliant rot of life.
All around the streaming bergs, men in kayaks
and umiaks take fish seldom seen so far north—
lumpsuckers and cod fleeing the warming,
deathly, central seas.

Somewhere in Greenland a furtive shadow falls
as the Green Man walks paths dim in memory,
calling forth blade and leaf, yet even he—
for whom green is all—stares confounded
at the ultimate cause of this riot of life.

On every hand, vessels greater than the greatest
gray whales converge, floating islands—
steel forests to his eyes—with roots that draw
black blood alone.

There is No Cure for Desire

Thwarted, it persists
> A young girl strikes matches
> one after another
> by an alley dumpster

Yielding, it persists
> Rain on the bus window
> bends as acceleration
> overcomes gravity

Denied, it persists
> Three agèd, black-robed priests
> sit in hoar tribunal,
> demand all her details

Fulfilled, it persists
> Creeks spill across the cracked
> drought-wracked plain
> as the vortex descends

Beneath the Bridge

Gentrification is not urban renewal.
—Sarge, on the San Antonio River

Beneath the bridge, battered heroes gather.
They wear their faded, frayed fatigues as if
merely place had changed—here they can share their
daymares with men whose limbs are just as stiff,
who weep with joy at the weather 'copter
who cringe at any sudden sound or shift
from light to shadow, who keep a proper
distance from feelings untouched by the swift
terrible absence of a comrade's face.
Beside the bridge a cypress tower stands—
a hollow haven, a place to embrace
both guilt and fear, old panic and new plans.
But now the holy haven's filled with brick
and what was healed again grows sick.

Southeast of the Center of Everything

Southeast of the center of everything
they are raping the volcanoes:
the prince and princess of Mexico,
Popocatépetl and Iztaccíhuatl,
Smoking Mountain and White Woman.
They are stripping away the green
gowns from the sleeping lovers,
leaving their flanks naked to the sun.

Two thousand years Popo has held his peace,
watched one sun follow another—
cuarto sol, quinto sol, sexto sol,
watched Aztec follow Toltec,
mestizo follow Spaniard.
He quenched his rage in molten stone;
she quenched her grief in virgin snow.

For centuries they slept undisturbed
beneath their mantles of green and white,
she in some cosmic absence, reclining
across a quarter of the horizon,
he fuming and restless, slowly
burning inside yet pleased to accept
the rainmakers' small offerings
of tobacco, chipotles,
copal-scented prayers.

But now the rainmakers
with their rattles and feathers
have themselves gone to ground
como las chicharras and there is no one
to honor los poderes más viejos,
to keep the cycles of water and life.
Popo rumbles in his long sleep
as the chainsaws and bulldozers
denude his lover's long limbs.

Beside the Dry Bed

Beside the dry bed of this brook
I read in drowsy, dying shade
as withered roots all softly groan
when once-stout limbs ache to incline

toward other valleys, other brooks;
but here I've settled with no blade
of green in sight, no seed unsown
to worry with, no sound or sign

of life or hope. Yet in the book
the story strays where I have strayed
in dreams where these meadows have grown
wild and drought is a daymare line

in ink that's paled past second looks.
Still, shadows cast by green-sleeved maids
that raise the flesh up from the bone
are dreams of dreams beyond our time

where all that's green is what we took
to tuck in books where grief is played
out page by dusty page. Alone
like some Baptist to whom no sign

is shown I stare beyond the brook
to the west—yes—some storm's displayed
and distant cat-eyed dice are thrown.
Below, there's rumbling in the mine.

A Dirty Business

It's a dirty business, this digging coal.
Ask the women who wash the sweat and dust
from black-caked coveralls and undershirts
gone gray beyond what bleach can touch but must
be daily wrung and hung in winds that etch
their window panes with the gray ghosts of those
who, lying restless in the groaning ground,
died dreaming of heavenly samite clothes.
Ask the women whose kisses fall each night
on faces grown gray and deeply grooved,
etched like lace by the acid-ink of coal.
Ask the orphans, ask the black-wrapped widows.
Ask those who gain the world and gladly lose . . .
We would dig anything else, could we choose.

Wings

"To fly's to live," she often said
at fifteen, showing the sling
with the broken arm that would
not be her wing.

Post cards came, always aerial
scenes or shots of sudden drops—
cliffs or canyons, a skyscraper,
a bell tower.

Then photos of her flying machines:
F-15s then the black wedge,
silent, stealthy, a bat's shadow
against the stars.

"To fly's to live," she often said
at thirty, showing the steel-
plastic-microchip miracles
that were her limbs.

On the impossibly high bridge
above the Rio Grande
she paused, left a pile of post cards,
each stamped and signed:

"To die's to fly."

Marching en las calles de la memoria

I know I was there, he said.
There's my face in the photos,
my phrasing in the manifestos.
It was all tweed and black turtlenecks
back when black was a statement
though it has never not been.

I know I was there, he said,
my hand on the presses that bled
raw revolution and cooked culture,
marching ahead of the marchers
churning out words that would
chant themselves tomorrow.

I know I was there, he said.
The paranoia struck deep and left
echoes of fear: narcs and moles
once comrades, trusted friends
who shared everything
in the purple haze of hope.

I know I was there, he said,
though what I say today eludes me
and the keyboard's become a maze
that coffee won't cure and
midnight will not illumine
though I know, I know

Detour

Poetry enters his world like a unicorn—
absurd beast, out of place and out
of time, yet undeniable as

the unforeseen detour: sudden
stacking tail lights, pale embers blown
dangerous and bright in the twilight.

Blood pounds against the change
of course, of expectation, of all
intention, and yet, there she is with her

slender silver horn, coat shimmering,
absorbing the failing light, and those
eyes that end momentum.

Once More I Come

For Mary; in memory of Peter S. Beagle

Once more I come, my winding through the hills
an old and cherished habit—take one lane
until it leads into another still—
seeking what I do not know, not quite sane,
not quite sober, intent on neither time's
passing nor its odd untroubling absence.
Once more I descend to the land of signs
and schedules, leaving behind the rich scents
and scenes that I would share with you alone
for only you and ours are worth the breach
of such sweet solitude, each hour its own
universe of stories: On the beach,
unicorns frolic in the froth—but some
lead us back to the hills from whence we come.

Nocturne for Bellsong and Train Horns

Last night the carillon sang of itself,
as it will when the evening winds befriend
the east-bound bats and the undampered brass
can hum unhammered, trending with the wind.

Beyond the bellsong, far trains rumble.

Two and one half miles exactly, southeast
of my pillow some Amtrak engineer
feathers his low horn like Coltrane easing
his way into some newborn melody.

So we enter the night. Evensong yields
to the nocturne sung by the silver trains
(holding back for the main act, as if
asking: Is anyone here? Anyone at all?)

Silence follows, dense and dark, and I slip
once more toward the borders of sleep when bells
break out—crossing bells now—less than a mile.
Chorded horns thrum loud, rising, insistent.

They demand: Are you there? And I reply
speaking to the night, speaking to the trains
as Samuel spoke to the Lord from his cave,
I am here.

Gray Descending

Today I take to the highway knowing
that this time no home waits ahead.

Befriending gray descends, comforting all
the dry cracked lands when drought-wracked streams

seem to swell as rain-scent enchants the plain.
Today I take to the highway

to sing of rain, the great gray gift that turns
these tawny pastures green again.

Ahead, gray descends, befriending all but
the ones who cannot see beyond

its dim and misty shroud. Today I take
to the highway to weep alone,

to weep aloud, knowing her hands are still,
cold, and gray. Ahead, gray descends,

befriending those who shun blue sky and sun.
Today I take to the highway.

II.

Take to the Highway

(Prose poems written at speed)

Take to the highway,
won't you lend me your name?
Your way and my way
seem to be one and the same.

—James Taylor, "Country Road"

Advent's End

Fog clogs the highway but clears the mind of all but the tail
lights wavering in and out of focus as distance and density
compete for attention with the black ice creeping across
the asphalt the further north you get, transiting both map and
memory as you recall another winter drive toward another death
bed fifty-six years ago, the night a cop pulled your father over
somewhere between Estilene and the bridge over the dry-as-
Ezekiel's-bones Prairie Dog Town Fork of the Red River for
speeding in a midnight blizzard, and it was only when you heard
your father explain that *his* father was dying that very night in
a hospital still a hundred miles away that your seven-year-old
self understood that all journeys can end without arriving at an
appointed end—just a slide and a thump, barely audible through
the downy snow-thick air, just a wheezing cough and a gasp, just
a glance away from the business of staying alive long enough to
earn a wistful moment or two of longing or regret or admiration
in the tumbled memories of those left behind, perhaps no more
than an image, enshrined in the mind for no apparent reason, like
that other winter night when you were too old to believe in Santa
but were determined to believe simply because you did not want
to not believe when you snuggled beneath your grandmother's
quilts (three deep—oh, we were quilt-rich back then) when at
the fringe of sleep you saw your father in the swirling white
cold beyond the rimed and rattling panes bringing in the gift
only Santa could bestow because only Santa could know and the
option of believing because you did not want to not believe was
abruptly null, your faith sucked into that void from which faith

in anything other than the present moment never returns without its twin shadows of guilt and doubt, shadows that cloud at once the meaning of yesterday and the potential of tomorrow as thoroughly as the fog clogs this highway yet lenses all time into momentary focus when you hear the dead calling you to breakfast from the kitchen on Christmas morning and you smell the sage and pepper-rich sausage your grandfather had slaughtered, butchered and smoked only weeks before, and grandmother's biscuits and turkey hash and the strawberry preserves made from your own labor the preceding spring when the ruby fruits stained your hands as if . . . and here speculation falters as memory stumbles, and you are parking your car in the hospice parking lot because yes, if you refuse to die in a corporation hospital they will be happy to rent you a room in which you can die at your leisure, and you lean back, exhausted by hours of hyper concentration, minding the road, fighting the ice, entering the ghostly vortices that envelop the car as if to enshroud it but engine heat keeps the pall from forming on the hood although snow begins to freeze on the windshield almost at once, so you hesitate to shut off the ignition, reluctant to leave because to quit the car is to quit the dream and to step again into the storm.

Strings

There's only one thing to say and even though you've worn it out over the thirty years he's been gone, you say it again, out loud in his own garage—good grief, Daddy, another tool box full of memories sharp as shrapnel that perforates the insulating years and you get that too-familiar feeling of a knight being killed with an old-fashioned can opener or a spider striving against the wind that first strips away the dew diamonds then shreds the web that was itself woven by instinct, the same kind of genetic instruction that fits your hands so perfectly to the worn wooden handles of wrenches and spanners made for Model Ts that rusted to dust half a century ago or pocket knives with scrimshaw rubbed to nothing and blades sharpened to slender crescents or exotic cherry-wood block planes that have shaved furniture and flutes, guitar necks and cat coffins, but emerge now from their own brass-hasped coffin, each wound in linen shrouds still scented with lemon oil and tied with his particular knot, a knot you study once again believing this may be the last time you will pull the string that unravels one of the perpetual mysteries of childhood. But you weren't expecting the tool box effect this time because this time it's your mother's chest of drawers you are emptying and sorting, sorting and emptying, and the treasures are merely familiar bracelets, broken watches and dangerously thin rings until you reach the triple-strand faux pearl necklace, Jackie's pearls, laid away on black velvet in the original black box, now yellowed and flaking like strings of ancient knobby teeth, as fragile as your mother's voice asking over and over, now, who are you?

Four-Stroke

If ever you spent much quality time on the hurricane deck of a trusted motorcycle then had to give it up—trading it in, say, for a station wagon to haul around your rock band or maybe pay a tuition bill or buy an engagement ring—then you'll recognize the symptoms of the syndrome: involuntary if slight twists of the wrist, muscle memory that leans into a curve, the tendency to roll down the car window with the A/C on, prompting your wife/kids/partner to ask if something is wrong—every time you pass a rider in your family minivan or SUV or silent little electric leaf blowing down the highway, and it dawns on you that you never really fell out of love with that old Honda 305 or the chopped metal-flake green Triumph 650 or even the minibike you built with your dad, with its angle-iron frame (that's how you learned to weld), its wheelbarrow tires, bicycle handlebars, and the 3.5 horsepower Briggs & Stratton four-stroke former lawn mower engine that your father insisted you must rebuild before he would even entertain the idea of letting you spend your allowance on a real centrifugal clutch, and so you spent weeks figuring out how to take it apart, washing each part in gasoline, and naming the parts—ah, the naming of parts: there seemed to be hundreds but it was only a few dozen—as you laid them out neatly on a sheet of cardboard on the garage floor: piston and rings and rod, camshaft and timing chain, valves and lifters, ball bearing races, carburetor needles and springs and floats and ports, and the beautiful gleaming crankshaft—and what was of importance to most third grade minds was simply blown away by the burning desire to know

the name and function of every part and to use the seemingly
ancient tools to bore the cylinder by hand, grind the valves
by hand, clean each carburetor orifice by hand, and replace
every part correctly in relationship to the others so that like
your father cleaning his rifle beneath a jeep on the beach at
Iwo Jima you could do it from memory in the dark, and your
father watched, advised and consoled you when it did not start
the first time or the second time or the fifteenth time you
took it apart and put it back together as third grade became
fifth grade until finally the magic of mechanics worked and
the engine roared and you danced a private jig in the twilight
of the garage to the rhythm the engine puttered, bolted to its
vibrating wooden base, as you sang "I've just seen a face, I can't
forget the time or place, where we just met" and you were star-
tled to find that you were as in love with that 3.5 horsepower,
four-stroke Briggs & Stratton engine as you ever were with the
girl with the Picasso pony tail who sat in the desk in front of
you the day Kennedy died and with whom no one could even
compare until you met the love of your life a decade later—*that*
kind of obsessive love, the kind that led you to copy out by
hand the *Encyclopaedia Britannica* article on trigonometry and
damn near memorize the thing while barely understanding it
just like you'd memorized the engine parts on the garage floor
or her pony tail on that cold November morning without a clue
as to what drove you to begin writing poetry that very day—
and when that kind of love was rewarded not only with the gift
of a shiny new centrifugal clutch but the consequent gift of
actual speed, as if you'd been gifted with the Wright Brothers'
wings, speed, solitary, wind-making, hair-whipping, jacket-
flapping speed, speed that would grow with one machine after
another just as the bonds with your father would dissolve in

the face of a war, so unlike his, that you could not agree to fight, speed that would carry you across deserts and mountains to the Haight, from Woody Guthrie to T.S. Eliot and back again, from the trinity of sex, drugs and guitars to that of blood, birth and the quietude you only glimpse now when the highway wind lashes eye and ear and arm as you watch some young man and his twenty-something old lady twist the throttle that churns the four stroke dream between his legs, accelerating, pulling away, leaving you with mere echoes of desire.

Eós and the Train Horns

I.

Dawning memory is tangled in its tellings, fractured into multiple perspectives, more than one of which could have been yours, so you remain unsure of exactly how far away the red and yellow Santa Fe Chief locomotive was when your grandfather yanked you off the tracks in front of his yellow and brown depot in White Deer, Texas. A few yards, a quarter mile? They tell you that you were two years old (there's most of the problem: whose memories are you remembering?) but you *know* you remember specifically placing two buffalo nickels on the hot iron track, to be flattened by the Chief. Or was it the Santa Fe El Capitan? Or are the crushed nickels later memories layered upon an earlier one? You remember the vibrations, the sun's glare on the silvered steel, the heat of the cinder bed and other . . . things that appear too closely observed: the rattlesnake dozing in the shade beneath the wooden loading platform, the twisted brown faces in the rust etching the cast iron wheels of a baggage cart with its curved oak handles worn smooth as glass, the tap-tap-tappeting of your grandfather's telegraph key, the rhythmic squeak of the speckled blue porcelain-on-metal Western Union sign swinging in the endless Panhandle wind, the painting of a Navaho bead maker on a fading Santa Fe calendar on the depot wall, the echo of your father's warbled whistling of an Edith Pilaf song—things too richly enshrined in the telling to have been true of the moment but which were certainly true of the time. And thus unravels your first living memory, leaving you to re-weave the tapestry of who you really are.

II.

Fifty years on and you awake as Eós tints the San Antonio sky;
you awake to a concert of train horns, surrounded, embraced in
your bed by the encircling sweep of familiar rumbling freights,
locomotives of shadow and steel crossing the still-dark streets
with their soft Spanish names—Guadalupe, Frio, Flores, Presa—
past the ghosts of long-gone stations that saw armies off to war
and welcomed generations of refugees from the wars across the
Rio Grande, pulling a hundred gondolas and tank cars and box
cars, some of them empty, open to the wind, singing their own
great hollow songs as they pound out a low echoing grumble
from downtown's last wooden trestle, when there enters another
strain: the one remaining passenger train rounding the center of
the city. Sharp braking squeals punctuate Amtrak's Air Chimes,
feathered by their engineer into a sweet tenor above the mel-
low baritone chords of Burlington Northern's old Nathan and
Leslie horns, instruments half a century old, all supported by the
thrumming mellifluous Primes of the Union Pacific and Santa
Fe freights. No rules of harmonization apply to this chorale
as mockingbirds and mourning doves join in the hymn to the
dawn. Swinging left at Carolina Street, headed north with their
increasing beat toward Sunset Station, locomotives serenade the
heart of the city, set the day in motion with lullabies and alarms,
lonesome moans and howls of joy—all rising with the memory of
that first train horn, bearing down on you, flying west across the
Panhandle plains, singing its warning song to the station master
in a tiny cattle town where you could have been crushed like
buffalo nickels beneath steel wheels, a brilliant but all too brief
smear of blood on the tracks.

III.

On a moonless night, a dark, dark night, running a steady 70
miles an hour along the banks of the Mississippi with city lights
dancing on the black waters, you stand between the cars of the
former Panama Limited, newly re-christened as the only-briefly-
discontinued City of New Orleans, tossing cigarettes into the
night and singing "The Train They Call the City of New Orleans"
with an old blue-suited, brass-buttoned conductor, while the old
E-8-A's and newer Pooch engines thrum down the rails from
Chicago to the Gulf. Closer to dawn, you bring hot chocolate to
your son, destined to stare at the sky for the rest of his life, and
together you struggle to see stars through the murky dome of the
observation car. The University of Chicago's gargoyles fall away as
a once-and-future place as you try to hold this moment, freeze
it, fix it even as you feel its edges fray, watch its colors fade like
a Polaroid left in the sun, until only the train songs and the stars
remain.

Leaning into the Learning Curve

Steel wheels turning, memories churning, time swoops in and
out of adolescence, landing you against the black wall at the back
of the tiny stage of The Attic Window—a Dallas coffeehouse/
bookstore with chess tables but no fantasy section—down off
Oak Lawn Avenue, armed with your father's banjo, clawing and
flailing—making it up—as Mike Ames, a Hell's Angel gone over
to the hippie side, blows pot smoke and irony from a cider jug
tied to a mic stand and beats hell out of an old guitar, singing
"I got the blues when my baby left me down by the Frisco Bay"
in a rusty tenor until Mickey Raphael launches into a raucus
"I'm a goin' fishin', mama goin' fishin', baby's goin' fishin' too"
then—selecting a harp from his Marine Band treasure chest, his
long fingers a minuet unto themselves—suddenly turns a lame
love song into sheer magic, blowing counterpoint melodies like
Larry Adler playing Gershwin, while Greg Fisher—long dead
now—strums along on a beat-up Martin and you are burning to
grab the guitar and wail out "Freight train, freight train, roll-
ing 'round the bend" when you realize—at that moment—that
you have no right to sing such a tune, realizing right then that
you "can't go back home this a-way" because it is not you who
really knows trains but your grandfathers and uncles, not you
who hoboed out of the Missouri mines to the Panhandle boom
towns, not you who swung lanterns in the dark switching yards,
coupling and uncoupling the wealth of America to send it rolling
across the country, not you who has any right to sing about the
holy humming of the steel rails or the lonesome whistles even if
they do inhabit your dreams, and so home you go that very night

to throw your paper route in the morning, leave a note—you'll be spending a couple of nights with a friend it says—and take off into the dawn, bound for glory or at least for a steep learning curve. It takes only a minute to hitch a ride with an early commuter, a hot young office girl headed to work in a pink miniskirt and nylons like sprayed-on armor. She drops you at the end of Harry Hines Blvd.—old 77—where it's easy to jump an open MKT box car as it rumbles and clanks and booms with the inertial shock that runs the length of the mile-long train as she begins to roll west. It is four days later when you call your Dad from Wichita, having arrived there via Fort Worth and Enid, Oklahoma. He smiles on the phone and wires you fifty bucks to come home in style on the Texas Chief—twelve dollars for the ticket, the rest for new jeans so your mom won't ask questions and a flannel shirt you will treasure for a decade. The next time you step on stage it's your song, not Miss Cotten's or Woody's. "It's a freight train morning, the kind that makes you want to ride" you sing and, Lord, what a ride it was. So that half a century later you lie in your bed, swaddled in the morning's concert, layered in sweet hymns of labor, mechanical and human, songs rising up like hawks looping into the sky, like Mickey's harp tangled with your father's warbling whistle. Once more you find these dark freights on the dream line, pulling away full of damaged souls, full of tellings and retellings, full of you and me. Here she comes, rumbling out of the moonrise, and you're quick to throw yourself through the doorway to paradise, letting her wheels crush these memories like coins on the tracks. No more questions, no more answers; nothing to do but to let her roll.

Down the road a bit in America

If you didn't own a Ford back in the day then likely you didn't
take those long rambling road-trip vacations to remote caverns
or hidden canyons or desert meteor crash sites, and so there
will not linger at the back of your memory a dusty adobe motel
with honest-to-god tumble weeds and windmill water thick
enough to chew, but rather the postcard visions of these same
places, painted in back-alley New York studios where big sky
sunsets and painted deserts came out just this side of psyche-
delic. But either way, whether the etched memory is real or
second-hand illusion, now, a few miles down the road from one
of America's more famous caverns, there is a rundown tourist
court.... Probably, just down the road from every geographic
or cultural oddity on the planet there is some equivalent of
the rundown tourist court—I mean, Lord, there's a souvenir
shack on top of Mount Sinai—but in America, generally a mile
or two down what was in the '30s a new two-lane blacktop
but is now a pot-hole pocked, disintegrating back road half a
mile or more off the smoothly sterile modern highway, up out
of the landscape will rise some raggedy remnant of the days
when being a tourist was a serious communal adventure, some
L- or U-shaped building made of the very soil it stands on,
lined with peeling, turquoise-painted door frames with illeg-
ible numbers, looking very much like some backwoods brothel
except that you're in the wrong state for that and besides, only
the goldenest of golden-hearted hookers would deign to make
a warm and welcoming getaway of such a place—and there
are not many of those ladies left (maybe there never were all

that many)—and with the wind whipping up a dust storm
in the distance that looks like sundown before the Ragnarök,
and your GPS spouting nonsense, and your cell phone that's
texting "are you kidding?" to your every inquiry—then that
place by the side of the road begins to have a certain appeal,
and you begin to think of yourself as a hollow-souled wanderer
about to meet Gabrielle Maple by the now-defunct gasoline
pumps where she will be reading Françoise Villon and you will
quote T.S. Eliot to her, or maybe its appeal is not Depression-
era romanticism at all, but simply the exotic absence of neon,
whatever, but you see a wavering light in the office window and
a rusted "vacancy" sign that's creaking a soprano solo above the
deep tenor hiss that is sand-blasting your windshield, and now
you don't really decide, but your hands turn the wheel of them-
selves and set the brake and turn the key, and you wonder if
there's coffee inside and just how gritty it is, and just how bad
the scorpions in the shower will be, and whether the silhouette
in the window can possibly match your imagination.

Freedom's Just Another Word ...

The lake was hardly a lake at all—smaller than Walden Pond—
but to Dallas boys in the green years after the droughts of the
50s had been broken, Bachman Lake was a small miracle of
perch and gar, paddleboats and canoes, pecans that fed a thou-
sand squirrels and filled pies unmatched in memory since, elms
that actually went gold in autumn and ancient oaks so tall that
from an upper limb with a slingshot you could hit the silver
bottoms of the DC-7s that sailed overhead to land at Love
Field—a place to hear old Black men turn time backwards with
harmonicas like lonesome locomotive whistles and voices that
came from the clodded black earth itself. But that was just the
public lake. The magic places were upstream, beneath the bluffs
where the rich folk lived, down in the tangled woods, the semi-
urban home of opossum and raccoon, owl and jay, and fishing
holes full of crawdads and catfish you could catch with a hook,
a string and a grasshopper, where secrets were told and futures
mapped and for a few lucky elders of the tribe, sex was discov-
ered all over again for the first time—or so it was reported on
heart-carved trees and by half-buried milky condoms—where
we, the younger grapevine-smoking philosophers, pondered
the inviolable female mystery who lived with her folks a stone's
throw away, and how best to live an entire life in the seven or
eight years left before we would surely die in the un-magical
jungles of Viet Nam—if the nukes we sheltered from beneath
our splintered school desks didn't get us first—and so we sang
that we were rocks, "fortresses deep and mighty" with the
same fervor as "Rock of Ages, cleft for me" on Sunday mornings,

41

Sunday nights and Wednesday evenings at the Mt. Zion Baptist Church. Thus the appeal of *Huck Finn*, read and re-read until our grapevine smokes became corncob pipes and our striped tee-shirts turned into ragged flannels and running away seemed the only rational option. The Trinity was no Old Man River but it ran to the sea and even if the Gulf coast was not the Beach Boys' Malibu, it was better than living as echoes of our parents' drudgery or accepting the Army's unalluring travel options, even if you did get to be a hero in the cemetery. And so we heeded the call of the river, gathering dry logs along the creek, spare 2x4s from unwatched construction sites, nails and rope and tools from anywhere, shaping our raft stocked with fishing tackle and Boy Scout cooking gear and Wonder Bread sandwiches and sling shots and all was well until it wasn't, when not one of your comrades, your fellow existentialist romantics—ah, those musketeers, "foundation deep somehow"—not one would join you for the midnight launch, no one to share the October stars glistening on the lake, no one to help rope and lower the raft over the spillway to the creek that led away to the Trinity, no one to see the curious eyes of skunks and muskrats in the swampy dark or the mystic static sparking of the red brick power plant, or smell the increasingly toxic vapors that rose from what you would later learn was one of the most polluted rivers in Texas, no one to see when dawn found you setting your bed-sheet sail in midstream and reeling in the only living fish in the river, a two-foot alligator gar, grilled over charcoal on the raft, no one to hold your head while you vomited him back into the stinking water, rippling its beautiful rainbow sheen of oil and pesticides and who knows what else, no one to see you weep with the realization that not even your poetry could protect you from your desire for this freedom.

Fugue sans fin

I.

There are circles you remember and circles you forget. These are the same circles, appearing and disappearing simultaneously with no trace of guilt between. Motion driven by gears within gears, forces within forces, down to the lonely electrons orbiting in their ancient impossible universes, each its own Vitruvian perfection, squaring impossible circles, defying language-based description, leaping in and out of existence, in and out of reality. There are circles you remember and circles you forget. These are the same circles: seasons patterned yet impatient. You are lazily pedaling infinite zeros in the middle of an empty childhood street, the north-south meridian of your life to that moment, pondering the interlacing strands of past and future, skimming the outer currents of a temporal vortex against the tug of generations gone toward the heart of the gravity well before you while the wind at your back fills heart-sails you did not know you had, shoving, impelling, urging a tangential path toward the stars that turn so slowly overhead, Orion throwing a leg above the autumn horizon, clambering into his winter sky while you lean into the slow wide turn that just keeps turning, feeling your bicycle wheels going round and round to the flap-rap-slap of playing cards clipped against its spokes while huge sycamore leaves spin crisp and golden on an invisible updraft in the failing light, dancing just as you did with the gypsy dust devils that skipped across granddaddy's August prairie, eyes shut tight, hoping to feel the lift, ever so slight, that might hurl you to Oz or Avalon or Valinor.

II.

Headed for sixty-five now, about to turn *that* corner, respected, balding but healthy—tobacco free at last, no longer living on coffee and whiskey—with assets in all the accounts that matter, and just then, driving down the highway savoring sweet memories, good music and a clear sky—just *then*—when your kids are finally having kids and completion fits you like a favorite sweat shirt, with the hills rising to the west, tenting the horizon with an open invitation to drive on and on, just then a deep sigh of satisfaction won't stop won't quit won't end and the air just goes out and out and won't come back and some hand you cannot see grips your heart and you hear a silence in your chest like you've heard nothing before until a roaring begins in your ears like the time you lay on the ground twenty feet from Led Zeppelin's ten-foot stack of amps and speakers and even clothing seemed to melt away leaving fleeting glimpses of delights that still cling to your memory like Botticelli's gentle Aura clinging to her handsome thunderstorm. There are circles you remember and circles you forget. These are the same circles. The roaring fades, the light dims, and you realize that your car is slowing, slowing, drifting left, and it is all you can do to guide it toward the median where you see yourself spinning around and around with a high school buddy on Highway One a lifetime ago, sliding to a gentle halt beside the blond California Godiva on her palomino pony and you rest your head on the steering wheel now as you did then and find that the hills are still rising, still inviting, closer now though less distinct and you yearn to smell their pine and highland sage. But there is no air, and between you and that green and distant haven lies a silent prairie of rippling buffalo grass, all tawny browns and yellows, desiccated stems bowing in wind-

44

driven sin waves that blueshift in the distance as whites and blues flood across the prairie, flickering beneath a brilliant moon, the same moon that long ago—haloed with echoed light one starry night—whispered such delightfully innocent secrets that they nearly killed you, and you feel a brisk wind tousle your long locks as it lifts the windshield high to shimmer in the white lunar light like a crystal sail that catches the breeze and impels you forward again and your hands grip the wheel again, now festooned with worn wooden knobs radiating from oaken spokes. The rudder responds, the course shifts, and you heave to, pondering how it is that Einstein was so often correct about time.

III.

There are circles you can't remember and circles you can't forget. These are the same circles, the very same circles, the gears within gears, the patterns beneath patterns. You grip the wheel and spin it, pitching caution to the fates to see what they will do with it, chanting with the mead-quaffing old scop who has taken your arm "gaeth a wyrd swa heo scel"* as Vergil leans against the mast intoning, "the only road I could have taken was the road I took,"** to which you reply "chaos drives but she will not steer" as you still the spinning wheel to turn the ship to a different shore than the wind would have and now the slap of the waves against your prow recalls the flap-rap-slap of your childhood bike and you rub the blur from your eyes to discern figures dancing along the shore, arms waving you in, and you can see a quay clearly now as light pours across the ocean from the sun rising at your back and you recognize the faces ashore—fathers and mothers and children, lovers and muses and so many unknown familiars,

45

all somehow proud that you have found their shore and not some other—and all that could not be forgiven simply fades away. There are circles you remember and circles you forget. These are the same circles.

———

* "Fate goes where she will." *Beowulf*

** "Non lì era altra via che questa per la quale i' mi son messo." Dante, *Purgatorio*, I: 62-63.

Beneath the Perseids

The pecan trees are bearing again, the first crop after several droughty years, and the young professionals intent on the gentrification of your near-downtown neighborhood can't stand the mess made by a generation of squirrels gone mad with the abundance of the heavy green-hulled nuts that they nibble and pitch, nibble and pitch, littering the late summer sidewalks with half-eaten mast and sounding like rimshots on century-old tin roofs, while weaker limbs, overborne and long untrimmed by their parvenu owners, creak and crack with any good evening breeze, crashing down on fences and cars, bringing out neighbors who've never actually met to say "insurance never pays for this kind of thing" and "Oh, look, isn't that the big dipper or something?"—being too young to remember when you could lie on a cot in these back yards—only half a mile from downtown—and watch to the accompaniment of bullfrog and coyote songs the hypostatic abstraction of the Milky Way's still light flowing across the dark August skies as Telstar raced by and fireflies and falling stars made whatever might be on the black & white television inside pale by comparison, and being that they cannot miss what they have never observed, the neighbors exit the evening heat to reenter their real worlds, air-conditioned and connected to everywhere but the here and the now that will only impinge again at 4 a.m. when the train horns begin to blow low and lonesome as the heavy freights pull in and the hollow box cars and empty gondolas head north again, rumbling across the city's last wooden trestle over its crooked little river and mapping a sonic geography in the mind, swaddling the neighborhood with layers of meaningful deep-throated tones that merge now with the dawn chorus of mockingbird and jay, cardinal and sparrow, accented by the dull drumming of green pecans on the roof.

The Fiftieth Face

So you are staring at the fifty faces—abstract figures really,
but they say faces—that are supposed to be discernible in the
soaring stained glass window before you, while you mindlessly
calculate the number of pieces of individual glass there are by
averaging the number your thumb can cover, or would cover
if you had the chutzpa to hold your arm out, artist-like, in the
middle of services but you don't—have the chutzpa *or* hold
your arm out artist-like—when you ask yourself what it means
when meaning itself begins to pale, not like facts vanishing
from one's aging memory, not like losing faith in long held
beliefs—whether or not those beliefs have any bearing on real-
ity—but when their sense of importance, their meaning, loses
its grip on those facts and beliefs and they begin to drift, hav-
ing lost what kept them stable, what made them adhere each
to each, what allowed a belief in an unproven god to coexist
on an equal footing with a belief in love or your father's ham-
mer or string theory or any kind of future at all, given that the
sun will eventually burn out and cease to glimmer through the
2,437 pieces of glass that you have just calculated make up this
one window with its fifty figures, those hidden and those obvi-
ous, those with faces and those without, all but one of whom
seem totally oblivious to your gaze—your gaze alone among all
the eyes of this congregation—and you see her mouth moving,
begging to be remembered, begging to be described because
here she is among all these forty-nine other hooded and dis-
torted saints and sinners crowded amidst the swirling tongues
of sun-fueled red and yellow and orange, whirling from cross

to cross to cross like the vortices of flame that lay down tunnels to hell in a forest fire but here supposedly lead one heavenward, skyward, upward anyway, beyond the faces and figures, beyond the cathedral itself, but gravity and the dizziness of flight bring you back to those lips, moving imperceptibly, silently begging to be remembered, begging to be given a name, to be given a meaning that will not be lost in some rambling rumination on a dateless Sunday morning but will last like Persephone's story, as good on one spinning planet as on any other.

A Desert Mountain Love Song

You knew the place for what it was the first and only time you
saw it—below the tree-line stand of aspen on the summit of
Mt. Livermore, where from a den of red-skinned madrones a
clear eight-mile sight line across the valley of the Limpia (dry
for decades but a chirping little stream in your earliest memo-
ries) revealed the gleaming twin domes, now a trio, atop Mt.
Locke—a place you knew no one but a lost coyote would ever
find you so you put an "x" on a map and took the coordinates
so that years later, which is to say yesterday, you could send
postcards to your daughter and your son on opposite ends of
the country saying simply "Look here when you have to. All
my love," after which you stole the keys to your caregiver's car
and lit out down the highway with just one small backpack, a
flask of Jameson's and the Colt peacemaker no one ever knew
you had—just in case the old bastard takes too long in com-
ing or the errant coyotes come too soon—and now you're here,
having ditched the car at dawn off 118 with a thank-you note
to its owner and hiked up the canyon—more arduous a task
than you imagined, but hell, you're on the downhill side of sev-
enty-eight (and what did you expect anyway?)—found the spot
curiously unchanged and cut the saplings to weave a lattice
couch to keep your ass off the ground and your eyes on the sky,
spread out your grandfather's four-stripe Hudson Bay blanket,
put on your hefty red Guatemalan shirt 'cause it gets cold out
here at night and besides, you told everyone that you would
be wearing it, and then the vest with all the kitschy patches
of all the places you've been with the love of your life and you

brush away the twinge of guilt over not lying down beside her back in the city but you know that when they gather up what's left of you when they find you that that's where most of your bones or maybe your ashes will end up, and you lie down on the couch, looking up at the wonderfully dark and brilliant sky, the darkest skies on the continent, exhausted by the drive and the hike and the cancer and it is all just as you imagined it would be, all as it should be, as you slip the blue bandanna over your head to keep your jaw from falling open in the long night because you remember the horror of your father's last gasp, wired and tubed and miserable, mouth gaping and nostrils flared, and you swore you wouldn't go that way, so here you are listening to the javelinas rooting in the brush and the rattlers winding in their lethal almost-silence among the boulders that glisten with quartz and rhyolite, and the occasional swoop of owl wings as the doors slide open atop Mount Locke and the silver-white dome turns in search of a planet where the air has not been fouled by its most intelligent vermin, and you crush the sage in your hand and put it to your nose, and wait "in the shadow of your own words" (as your first good song put it so long ago) and you wish you had your old Martin with you now, but one of the kids would want it so you left it but you can still feel its music in your hands like you can still feel your love's breasts and hips and hair of sixty years back, and you pray that if there's anything at all beyond the veil, it will be her voice calling your name.

III.

All That Would Be

Rekindling

And so we departed
from the season
of that haloed moon
with our child-like wonder
intact, frozen
like the crystals that caught
and shattered that light.

Spring moons bled
and fled from what seemed
some temporal rift
as we observed the fall
of all we deemed
real, substantial,
watched a new
species of fear evolve.

Wonder unjaded, we stared
stared as August's moon
stubbornly hung
pale but full
above the sunrise,
as reluctant as we
to fade into the light.

Once paired pilgrims
we watch tonight
for the passing
of autumn's new moon
riding astride Orion's thigh
as we cross Halley's dusty trail
and the heavenly sparks fly.

We seek the rare fires
that streak behind
the black absence
and reappear,
twice-born meteors,
as we cautiously
rekindle one memory
at a time.

Constellations

In the pine paneled room,
after the change he began
to name the constellations

of knotted brown stars
that ranged across his walls,
undulations swelling

the rich wooden sky
from two-dimensional planes
into the contours of memory

and he finds her form
grown phosphorescent
against the imagined sky.

On the table: a blackened
fragile rose,
just showing green.

All That Would Be

I would that we could celebrate continuance,
the putting of one foot before another, the drawing
of one more breath, inhaling the fragrant piñon

in high passes where our paths never crossed
and never will except in these highway idylls
wherein the contours of the eroded mesas

become—if only from one angle—a perfect profile,
as if you lay sleeping all across the horizon and my eyes,
being male, can focus on nothing else.

I would celebrate continuance: watching for the small
but regular marvels—invisible ice that rings the moon
with echoed light, the glowing spheres

that dance upon Chinati's windy heights,
the desert spring that flows clean and free but
will never reach the sea—had you not declared

all that had been to be all that would be.
I would that we could celebrate continuance
beyond the borders of sorrow.

It Was Ever Illusive

for Mary

It was ever illusive,
a hawk lost in the sun
for the moment but never
the object of the day,
which was to multiply

the day itself, preparing
these hatchlings for their
solos into the sun, out
of sight but never
out of mind. So now

we stare north and east
for their bright plumage
to come winging home
or simply to pass safely
from sunlight to shadow.

Sun-blind, my eyes
rest on you once more,
and I know that what
there is or ever was to find
I will find only here.

The Last Halloween

for Brigid

The Christmas tree is a brittle
brown skeleton by the back fence
before the autumn photographs,
belated leaves of memory,
fall from the drugstore envelopes
and we gather around to see
how the camera caught us.

What I notice first are the missing:
There is no scarecrow picture
for there was no scarecrow sitting
in the red metal chair this year
and the birthday pictures
are just that, records of marker
moments, cake and candles.

Here I am planting a pine in the yard
and I wonder if someday someone
will stand beneath it, showing this
photograph to a small child, saying
"He loved trees, he did."
Like the scarecrow, I will be a squeakless
memory in the rusted metal chair.

Enough pathos I think, and listen
as my daughter critiques her Halloween

costume—something did not go with
something else—when I see what I saw
through the lens and tried to forget:
my princess, chin in palm, dreaming
full sail beside the jack-o-lanterns,
dreaming of her somewhere-prince,
knowing that this dark evening
with its perfect yellow moon
was the last that she would wander
as a child, free as the gypsy
she had chosen to be, bejeweled
in borrowed finery again.

His Numbered Mind

for Michael

Inside
his numbered mind
decisions rest
on intuitions
springing
from the deep logic
that stacks cards
with assurance
and not wonder
yet
he holds wonder
like an ace
confident
ready to be played
when logic comes up
short
and only wonder
will do

When I wander
inside
his numbered mind
I am lost
in wonder

Where Time Has Lost Its Way

After W.B. Yeats' "The Stolen Child"

Where to find in these late days
a human child to steal away?
To hear our sweet beguiling,
our songs like flowers smiling,
our beckoning to heed
and, reckoning no need
to fear our faery greeting:
Come, oh come, oh come away
where time has lost its way.

Where to find in these late days
such a child to steal away?
Our poetry is dying
and all around us sighing,
our wildlings now know grief
—the hours grow so brief—
How to inspire believing?
Come, oh come, oh come away
where time has lost its way.

Where to find in these late days
a human child to steal away?
We need their love and loathing,
their dreaming and supposing,
need them to abhor us,
wish on and adore us.

Now from the void a chorus:
Come, oh come, oh come away
where time has lost its way.

Where to find in these late days
a child whose faith will let us stay
in flowery hidden bowers
where dancing between hours,
we weave the sweet beguiling,
the longing for lands lying
beyond the fields you know, but now
we go, we go, we go away
where time has lost its way.

Trout and salmon steal away,
their thought and speech are lost today.
Moonlight falls on silent lawns
empty now of sprite and faun.
The young streams have grown old,
the water rats grown bold.
Deaf to magic, deaf to fear,
no human child will ever hear:
Come, oh come, oh come away!

Now, we . . .

for Naomi

With so much in common, we are
so far from our fathers now
and we . . .

seek pecan-shaded memories—
children and streets (empty now)
that we . . .

meet only by appointment
or at the post office now
where we . . .

mention matters of consequence—
our mothers are dying now
while we . . .

have become references
rather than prodigals now
that we . . .

are Palestinian prickly pear
and Texas blackthorn now
icons we

never intended.

Icons

And on this wall are the icons.
No, not religious—unless writing
is a religion.

Here's Alice
at ten, dressed as a beggar
with one nipple barely showing.
Handwritten poems by
my betters and a letter
with a photo of an old man
with his briar
and his blackthorn.

Here's a tequila flask,
carefully preserved,
said to have been handed
to General Villa to toast
some soldadera for bravery
or beauty.

And here's a girl
hugging an old guitar,
                    suspended
at an intersection of time
and the timeless.

Here's my father's pipe,
inscribed with his battle sites—Iwo,

Wake, and the one that killed him
years later—Nagasaki.

What? No, none
are religious. Well,
maybe
one.

The Watch

for Maxine

Once she began to slip away
her sterile chamber blossomed
and rainbows graced the gray
and futile prayers of petition
as sodden hymns grew wings
(once she began to slip away)
elegant as her ancient pearls,
so rich in remembrance
that rainbows graced the gray
loss that loomed so large,
tinting her snowy canvas
(once she began to slip away)
with pale shades and echoed light
—lunacies from beyond the storm
of rainbows that graced the gray.
The light that was was gone;
the light that was dawned again
once she began to slip away
and rainbows graced the gray.

Anything More

for Maxine

You've been asleep for weeks
but the morphine
won't work any more

and your sister and brother
and parents—shadows so
long at your door—

have all gone their ways
and you can't say what
you're waiting for,

stretch out your hands
to that bit of light
beginning to bore

through the wall of your night.
I can't promise you
anything more

than this headlamp of an old train
emerging from the midnight plains
of all you knew before.

Witness

Here, where I must needs reside
beside this sea of silent dreams,
I have borne witness to such scenes
—beyond my paltry power to explain—
that I can only see and say:
"Here where I must needs reside
upon this shore occurred these things."
I will not weary the unwary with demons
(I have borne witness to such scenes)
or angels, or a deaf god who yet
grants us the grace of self-slaughter.
Here, where I must needs reside
I choose to sing of her alone,
of love beyond any bloated heaven.
I have borne witness to such scenes
and may not say what any might mean
beside this sea of silent dreams.
Here, where I must needs reside
I have borne witness.

Knots

Let it go, you told me, let go
of all the knotted reasons
that keep the story's thread
from going where it will,
catching on each branch
or stone I pass, pulling
me from the chosen path.

Let it go, I told myself, let this be
the season of exploration and yet,
foot-loose in this labyrinth
where memories grow rank beside
image-blooms unlived,
I miss the tedious business
of unraveling the knots.

In Aura's Garden

Some garden witch gathers, even now,
her fragrant or savory summer survivors,
the last green leaves of the last green bough

before ploughing under those she must—
her sweet spring memories now gone to dust.
Some garden witch gathers, even now,

autumnal rosemary, sturdy remembrance:
an old love, sifted by circumstance,
a last green leaf on the last green bough.

In the wildwood beyond we pine to share
her manicured miracles, but there, where
this garden witch gathers, even now,

so many secrets she will never bequeath
she beds her hyacinth bulbs beneath
the last green leaves of the last green bough

to erupt in a maze of purple plumes.
She has woven spring's sorrow upon her loom.
Some garden witch gathers, even now,
the last green leaves of the last green bough.

Waiting for the Tow

The day is severed:
planned from unplanned,
necessary from
necessary now.

Ripples run through it
bumping meetings,
edging off center
events that were

anticipated,
so finely balanced
that some loose screw
has set all askew.

Earning the Myth

Veterans of circumstance in opposing camps,
beyond the field where we were bruised and gashed,
I ask again: have we earned our myth?

We treated for peace beside the stream
where salmon dream, but they knew us for
veterans of circumstance in opposing camps,

and so submerged, hazel-wise but wordless,
powerless perhaps to answer the question
I ask again: have we earned our myth?

The salmon stare sightless now, poisoned
by those who chose to be deaf, themselves now
veterans of circumstance in opposing camps.

They trample the wheat from gold to ashen gray,
hurl stones at this lyre they can never play, and
I ask again: have we earned our myth?

They loved us well alone, but could not bear to see
the forest and castle in league. Of these
veterans of circumstance in their opposing camps,
I ask again: have we earned our myth?

Reach Out

When the streetlight people
    appear
like shadows ebbing in
and out of substance—more
or less tidal forms
of consciousness—
and their fingers graze
your desires
    leaving
your dreams crazed
like china teacups you cannot
bear either to shatter and discard
or simply pitch
    into oblivion
(because even shards
carry memories—yours
and theirs—into the unknown
    future
where someone no doubt
will know who you
    really were),
before their flickering
    existence
fades to static

reach out

Hallowed

I.

Everyone who knew Mead
acknowledged it:
Mead was a witch.

Hippie girls with a taste for
crystals and dulcimers
and chamomile tea

were hardly weird sisters
but when Mead waded
out into the mountain storm,

took the trail to the cliff-top
boulder, shed her clothes
and began to chant

and twirl, gathering
a glowing blue cocoon
of St. Elmo's fire

I began to suspect that indeed
Horatio's philosophy fell
a good deal short of the task.

II.

Many's the storm
I've stepped outside,
presented a good target,
drenched and alone,

and begged aloud
by a hallowed name
to be struck—
a fair exchange:

one lightning bolt
for a nanosecond
of conscious belief
(not proof)

that you exist
and hear.
I'm still here;
the offer's still good.

Necessary Work

From the making of harps
to the making of houses
he turned his hands to what
needed doing, to what
needed time and attention:

building a house to live in
building a house to die in

Each smashed finger
each bit of flesh taken
by saw or blade or chemical
took a bit of the music
out of his hands,
crippling what was there
for the making.

Mahogany Blues

I have caressed this mahogany neck,
these strings that sing and shimmer
above the ebony, grooved deep beneath
taut steel and the callused fingers
of all the bluesmen who made
love to her through the long
boxcar nights when she sang
alone above the thrumming steel,
and through those long duets
when her lover's lovers
drank in her blue soul.

I have caressed this mahogany neck
wrung out that one blue note
so sweet, so high
it hangs above the room
and will not resolve, will not settle
into this chord or that, major or minor,
will not grow or diminish but
leaves an absence in the mind
leaves the desire for the desire
for the return of an echo
you know is there but
cannot hear.

Reduced to Words Redux

A decade beyond
the last contact—we were still
stone and stonecutter—
I'm unsure who was the stone
and who wielded the chisel.

Here, now, we find
imitations of your too-perfect
breasts cut from stone
after stone, curves that fit
palms like a ciborium.

The real work was not
the carving but the calming
of my memory,
stilling forms that were so free.
Exhausted, I am reduced

to words alone.
Pen in hand, chafing fingers,
I await the lust
in language that was so warm
in the chisel, in the stone.

Intersection

Something stills the flight
of moments like a film caught
on a sudden single image

slightly askew, one
frame shaken by the
ratcheting projector

focusing all our eyes
on some thing—unnoticed
in the image stream until

something stills the flight
of these single moments
as when someone kills

the lights and a sudden after-
image hangs in the mind like
a cubist projection

of substance and motion:
the still center
that drives the dance

Mere Physics

In the mirror, October
ripens blotched with orange.
Summer cheeks
ruddy with laughter
fall like autumn's crown
as the blue above
goes gray with mist.

Thus do we conclude
with the largest metaphors,
those more subtle reserved
to parse younger hearts,
probe questions beyond
the mere physics
of gods and gravity.

Yellow lamp light, a mellow lute,
old poems in leather books,
a drift of leaves against the house,
singing skies gone still
as mists that dim
both eye and mind
fill October's mirror.

Gunshots in the night
fail to perturb and yet
disturb by that very fact.

Thus do we conclude.
Chance carried us
so far. The trembling
begins in the empty mirror.

Acknowledgments

I am grateful to the editors of the following journals and anthologies in which some of these poems have appeared:

"Advent's End" in *Southwest Review* (Winter 2014); also in *The Texas Weather Anthology* (Lamar University Press, 2016).

"All That Would Be" in *World English Poetry*, edited by Sudeep Sen (Dhaka: Bangladesh, 2015).

"Another Visitation" in *A Ritual to Read Together: Poems in Conversation with William Stafford* (Woodley Press, Sept. 2013) and in *HOT!* (Bihl Haus Arts, 2014).

"Beneath the Perseids" in *Clover*, No. 6, 2013.

"Beside the Dry Bed" in *Festschrift for Wendy Barker*, edited by Catherine Kasper (UTSA Creative Writing Program, 2014).

"Desert Mountain Love Song" in *The Asheville Poetry Review*, 20th anniversary issue, Nov. 2014.

"Down the Road Bit in America" in *Clover*, No. 4, 2012.

"The Fiftieth Face" in *Clover*, No. 5, 2013.

"Four-Stroke" in *Cutthroat: A Journal of the Arts* (No. 17, online edition, Summer 2014) and in *Far Out: Poems of the '60s* (edited by Wendy Barker and Dave Parsons, Wings, 2016).

"Gray Descending" in *The Texas Weather Anthology* (Lamar University Press, 2016).

"The Green Man Returns to Greenland" in the 2012 *Round Top Poetry Festival Anthology*.

"His Numbered Mind" in *Clover*, No. 8, December, 2014.

"The Last Halloween" in *Cutthroat: A Journal of the Arts* (Vol. 4, No. 1, Spring 2008) and in *The Best of Cutthroat* (Spring 2016).

"Lost Lines" in *San Antonio Express-News*, July 8, 2007.

"Rain in Due Season" and "All That Would Be" in *Clover*, No. 7, June 2014.

"Siduri" in *Clover*, No. 8, December, 2014.

"Strings" appeared in an altered form as "Knots and Pearls" in *Anglican Theological Review* (Spring 2015).

"Virginia Pines" in *San Antonio Express-News,* 2007, and in *Cutthroat: A Journal of the Arts* (Vol. 4, No. 1, Spring 2008).

"West of Lampasas" in *The Texas Observer* (September 2014).

ONLINE

"Another Visitation," "Southeast of the Center of Everything," "The Fiftieth Face," "Continuance," "Marching en las calles de la memoria" (under the title "Rehashing"), "Wings," "Beside the Dry Bed," "The Green Man Returns to Greenland," and "Down the road a bit in America," appeared in *World Poetry Portfolio #56: Bryce Milligan,* edited by Sudeep Sen (Molossus Press & *Atlas Magazine,* June 2013) — http://www.molossus.co/poetry/world-poetry-portfolio-56-bryce-milligan/

"Reduced to Words Redux" and "The Fiftieth Face" reprinted in *Kyso Flash* (http://www.kysoflash.com/Current.aspx), Oct. 1, 2014. http://www.kysoflash.com/ContentsIssue1.aspx#TopContent

Many thanks to my compatriot of many years, Roberto Bonazzi, first reader for much of my recent poetry. Thanks also to Rosemary Catacalos, Glover Davis, Clare Dunkle, Donald Hall, Jim LaVilla-Havelin, Edward Hirsch, David Lee, Barry Lopez, Naomi Shihab Nye, Dave Oliphant, William Pitt Root, Carmen Tafolla, Pamela Uschuk, Wang Ping and others who have commented on early drafts of some of these poems. Special thanks to John Crawford, publisher of West End Press, a comrade who still believes that words can change the world—thanks for asking for this book. I am also grateful and honored to have such fine writers on the back cover: Jane Hirshfield, Lorna Dee Cervantes, Juan Felipe Hererra, Stephen Harrigan, and David Lee. *¡Mil gracias!*

Without any doubt, my most heartfelt thanks go to my wife, Mary, who has made my life so rich. Forty years is just a start.

A Note on Method (if not craft)

For much of my life, friends have expressed concern over the fact that I write while driving, as well as curiosity regarding the mechanics of the process. I would advise young writers against this practice; it is, however, a skill like any other, and I seem to have mastered it. The fact is, a great many first drafts of my poems and songs of the past 45 years were composed while in motion—in a car, generally alone, almost always on smaller highways with limited traffic. I am grateful that this is not true of longer fiction.

I use a board, anchored at elbow-level, which functions as a moderately stable writing desk and I have, over time, learned to write without looking at the paper. Under-employed graphologists, epigraphers, or palæographers may find of interest the considerable number of yellow pads, generally containing a dozen lines or less per page, to be found in my archives at the University of Texas at San Antonio.

As it happens, the prose poems in *Take to the Highway* were all composed between August 2012 and June 2015 on Texas Highway 281, mainly between Blanco and Hico, Texas. I have no explanation for this except that my mother (the dedications to "Maxine" are for her) was dying and reviving throughout this period. Driving under these psychologically tense conditions allowed, I assume, the emergence of so many deep memories.

I call these pieces "prose poems" only for lack of a more precise term, and because that is what others have called them. They are certainly not "flash fiction." Nor are they, as Charles Simic defined the form, "a burst of language following a collision with a large piece of furniture." The roots of the modern prose poem supposedly lie in the French Symbolists, though I make no pretense that I have derived any "rules" to follow from Mallarmé or Baudelaire.

85

I have been asked fairly often to write an autobiography. This is, perhaps, an occupational hazard of being a good story teller. As a small press editor, critic, and literary organizer, I can see that there might be some interest in a literary memoir simply to document a time and place, but I fail to see that anyone would benefit from a more general endeavor to recount my life. Perhaps the prose poems in this collection will satisfy those few who want to know more than they can glean from my other works.

Finally, a word about the subtitle of this little book. The term "arabesque," whether in art, music, or dance, seems most often to be about capturing motion within patterns—intertwined leaf and vine motifs; melodic undulations sweeping across a score; the moment that pauses the flow of a ballerina—the moment that focuses energy into form. I use the term in relation to these poems in that sense, not the more-or-less hallucinatory sense implied by Gogol or Poe. As for the "travelers" of the subtitle, well, aren't we all?

About the Author

Bryce Milligan is an author working in numerous genres, from children's books to novels for young adults, to adult poetry and criticism. *Bloomsbury Review* once called him a "literary wizard." Critic Paul Christensen wrote of Milligan as "one of the principal writers of the region and a force at the center of the literary art movements of Texas." James Hoggard, past president of the Texas Institute of Letters once wrote of him as being "supremely successful in fostering both a public awareness and involvement in the humanities in Texas."

Milligan was the book columnist for the *San Antonio Express-News* and the *San Antonio Light* throughout the 1980s and early '90s. A member of the National Book Critics Circle, PEN American Center, and the Texas Institute of Letters, his reviews and essays appeared in many journals and newspapers, including the *New York Times*, the *Los Angeles Times*, the *Chicago Tribune*, the *Dallas Morning News*, et al.

The founding editor of *Pax: A Journal for Peace through Culture* (1983-1987) and (with Roberto Bonazzi) *Vortex: A Critical Review* (1986-1990), he directed the Guadalupe Cultural Arts Center's literature program and its San Antonio Inter-American Book Fair and Latina Letters conferences for several years. Milligan has been the publisher, editor and book designer of Wings Press since 1995. Wings Press has been profiled in numerous publications, including *Poets & Writers Magazine* and the *Huffington Post*. Ramón Renteria, *El Paso Times* Book Editor, wrote that, "Without publishers like Milligan's Wing Press, Latino and Chicano literature would remain in a deep well in America."

Milligan was the primary editor of *Daughters of the Fifth Sun: A Collection of Latina Fiction and Poetry* (Riverhead, 1995)—which was the first all-Latina anthology to be published by a major American publishing house—and *Floricanto Si: A Collection of Latina Poetry* (Penguin, 1998). He has edited several smaller anthologies and critical collections, and designed numerous books for other presses.

Milligan is the author of four historical novels and short story collections for young adults. *With the Wind, Kevin Dolan* (1987) received the Texas Library Association's Lone Star Book Award. One of his children's books, *Brigid's Cloak,* was a 2002 "Best of the Year" pick by both the Bank Street College and *Publishers Weekly.* Several of his gallery theater pieces have been produced weekly at the Witte Museum of Natural History in San Antonio for over 30 years.

Milligan is also the author of six previous collections of poetry. His poetry and his song lyrics have appeared in numerous literary magazines, including *Southwest Review, Asheville Poetry Review, Cutthroat, Clover, Texas Observer,* among others.

Once upon a time, he was a working luthier and a singer/songwriter. He has taught English and creative writing at every level, including workshops from California to Prague.

In 2011, he received the Gemini Ink "Award for Literary Excellence." In 2012, he received the St. Mary's University President's Peace Commission's "Art of Peace Award" for "creating work that enhances human understanding through the arts." In 2015 and 2016, the San Antonio Public Library and Bihl Haus Arts mounted exhibitions in celebration of Wings Press and Milligan's book designs.

More information at www.brycemilligan.com